HAL•LEONARD®

VIOLIN
PLAY-ALONG

AUDIO
ACCESS
INCLUDED

Lindsey Stirling
HITS

T0071730

CONTENTS

To access audio visit:
www.halleonard.com/mylibrary

Enter Code
7751-1203-1532-8986

ISBN 978-1-4803-6066-2

HAL•LEONARD®
CORPORATION

7777 W. BLUEMOUND RD. P.O. BOX 13819 MILWAUKEE, WI 53213

For all works contained herein:
Unauthorized copying, arranging, adapting,
recording, Internet posting, public performance,
or other distribution of the printed or recorded music
in this publication is an infringement of copyright.
Infringers are liable under the law.

Visit Hal Leonard Online at
www.halleonard.com

Cover photo: Tony Felgueiras

Jon Vriesacker, Violin
Audio Arrangements by Steven Tanner
Audio Arrangement for "All of Me" by Andrew Horowitz
Produced and Recorded by Jake Johnson at Paradyme Productions

All of Me

Words and Music by John Stephens and Toby Gad
Arranged by Lindsey Stirling

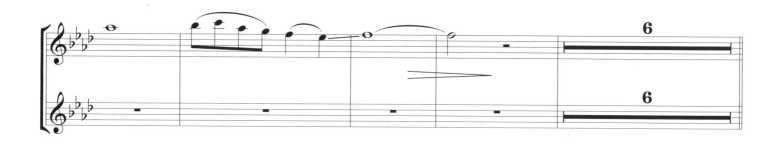

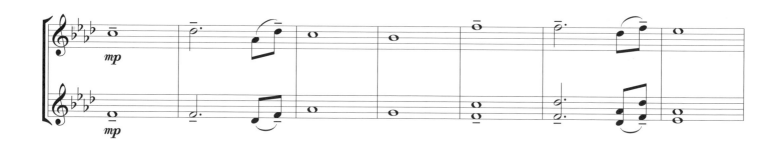

Copyright © 2013 John Legend Publishing, EMI April Music Inc. and Gad Songs, LLC
All Rights for John Legend Publishing Administered by BMG Rights Management (US) LLC
All Rights for EMI April Music Inc. and Gad Songs, LLC Administered by Sony/ATV Music Publishing LLC, 8 Music Square West, Nashville, TN 37203
All Rights Reserved   Used by Permission

All of Me

Words and Music by John Stephens and Toby Gad
Arranged by Lindsey Stirling

Copyright © 2013 John Legend Publishing, EMI April Music Inc. and Gad Songs, LLC
All Rights for John Legend Publishing Administered by BMG Rights Management (US) LLC
All Rights for EMI April Music Inc. and Gad Songs, LLC Administered by Sony/ATV Music Publishing LLC, 8 Music Square West, Nashville, TN 37203
All Rights Reserved   Used by Permission

All of Me

Words and Music by John Stephens and Toby Gad
Arranged by Lindsey Stirling

Copyright © 2013 John Legend Publishing, EMI April Music Inc. and Gad Songs, LLC
All Rights for John Legend Publishing Administered by BMG Rights Management (US) LLC
All Rights for EMI April Music Inc. and Gad Songs, LLC Administered by Sony/ATV Music Publishing LLC, 8 Music Square West, Nashville, TN 37203
All Rights Reserved   Used by Permission

Fix You

Words and Music by Guy Berryman, Jon Buckland, Will Champion and Chris Martin
Arranged by Lindsey Stirling

Copyright © 2005 by Universal Music Publishing MGB Ltd.
All Rights in the United States Administered by Universal Music - MGB Songs
International Copyright Secured   All Rights Reserved

Don't You Worry Child

Words and Music by Steve Angello, Axel Hedfors, Sebastian Ingrosso, Michel Zitron and Martin Lindstrom
Arranged by Lindsey Stirling

Copyright © 2012 UNIVERSAL MUSIC PUBLISHING AB, SONY/ATV MUSIC PUBLISHING UK LIMITED,
LATERAL MGMT LONDON STOCKHOLM AB and BMG CHRYSALIS SCANDINAVIA AB
All Rights for UNIVERSAL MUSIC PUBLISHING AB in the U.S. and Canada Controlled and Administered by
UNIVERSAL - POLYGRAM INTERNATIONAL PUBLISHING, INC. and UNIVERSAL - SONGS OF POLYGRAM INTERNATIONAL, INC.
All Rights for SONY/ATV MUSIC PUBLISHING UK LIMITED Administered by SONY/ATV MUSIC PUBLISHING LLC, 8 Music Square West, Nashville, TN 37203
All Rights for LATERAL MGMT LONDON STOCKHOLM AB Administered by KOBALT SONGS MUSIC PUBLISHING
All Rights for BMG CHRYSALIS SCANDINAVIA AB Administered by CHRYSALIS MUSIC GROUP INC., A BMG CHRYSALIS COMPANY
All Rights Reserved   Used by Permission

Good Feeling

Words and Music by Arash Pournouri, Tramar Dillard, Tim Bergling, Lukasz Gottwald,
Henry Walter, Pearl Johnson, Etta James, Leroy Kirkland and Breyan Isaac
Arranged by Lindsey Stirling

© 2011, 2012 EMI MUSIC PUBLISHING SCANDINAVIA AB, EMI LONGITUDE MUSIC CO., PRESCRIPTION SONGS, LLC,
DREAM MACHINE CORPORATION, KASZ MONEY PUBLISHING, SONY/ATV MUSIC PUBLISHING LLC,
ARTIST 101 PUBLISHING GROUP and INTERNATIONAL MUSIC GROUP, INC. BMI PUB DESIGNEE
All Rights for EMI MUSIC PUBLISHING SCANDINAVIA AB in the U.S. and Canada Controlled and Administered by EMI BLACKWOOD MUSIC INC.
All Rights for PRESCRIPTION SONGS, LLC, DREAM MACHINE CORPORATION and KASZ MONEY PUBLISHING Controlled and Administered by
KOBALT MUSIC PUBLISHING AMERICA, INC.
All Rights for SONY/ATV MUSIC PUBLISHING LLC Administered by SONY/ATV MUSIC PUBLISHING LLC, 8 Music Square West, Nashville, TN 37203
All Rights for ARTIST 101 PUBLISHING GROUP and INTERNATIONAL MUSIC GROUP, INC. BMI PUB DESIGNEE Administered by
WARNER-TAMERLANE PUBLISHING CORP.
All Rights Reserved   International Copyright Secured   Used by Permission

My Immortal

Words and Music by Ben Moody, Amy Lee and David Hodges
Arranged by Lindsey Stirling

© 2003 BMG RIGHTS MANAGEMENT (IRELAND) LTD., ZOMBIES ATE MY PUBLISHING and FOR THE FALLEN PUBLISHING
All Rights Administered by CHRYSALIS ONE SONGS and BMG RIGHTS MANAGEMENT (US) LLC
All Rights Reserved   Used by Permission

Pokémon Theme

Words and Music by T. Loeffler and J. Siegler
Arranged by Lindsey Stirling and Kirt Hugo Schneider
Tamara Loeffler & John Siegler

Copyright © 1999 Pikachu Music (BMI)
Worldwide Rights for Pikachu Music Administered by BMG Rights Management (US) LLC
International Copyright Secured   All Rights Reserved

Radioactive

Words and Music by Daniel Reynolds, Benjamin McKee, Daniel Sermon, Alexander Grant and Josh Mosser
Arranged by Pentatonix and Lindsey Stirling

Copyright © 2012 SONGS OF UNIVERSAL, INC., IMAGINE DRAGONS PUBLISHING, ALEXANDER GRANT and JMOSSER MUSIC
All Rights for IMAGINE DRAGONS PUBLISHING and ALEXANDER GRANT Controlled and Administered by SONGS OF UNIVERSAL, INC.
All Rights Reserved   Used by Permission

Star Wars Medley

Music by John Williams
Arranged by Lindsey Stirling and Peter Hollens

STAR WARS (MAIN THEME)
from STAR WARS, THE EMPIRE STRIKES BACK and RETURN OF THE JEDI
Music by John Williams

MAY THE FORCE BE WITH YOU
Music by John Williams

STAR WARS (MAIN THEME)
© 1977 (Renewed) WARNER-TAMERLANE PUBLISHING CORP. and BANTHA MUSIC
All Rights Administered by WARNER-TAMERLANE PUBLISHING CORP.
All Rights Reserved   Used by Permission

MAY THE FORCE BE WITH YOU
© 1980 WARNER-TAMERLANE PUBLISHING CORP. and BANTHA MUSIC
All Rights Administered by WARNER-TAMERLANE PUBLISHING CORP.
All Rights Reserved   Used by Permission

THE THRONE ROOM (AND END TITLE)
from STAR WARS: EPISODE IV - A NEW HOPE
Music by John Williams

THE IMPERIAL MARCH (DARTH VADER'S THEME)
from THE EMPIRE STRIKES BACK - A Twentieth Century-Fox Release
Music by John Williams

THE THRONE ROOM (AND END TITLE)
© 1977 (Renewed) WARNER-TAMERLANE PUBLISHING CORP. and BANTHA MUSIC
All Rights Administered by WARNER-TAMERLANE PUBLISHING CORP.
All Rights Reserved   Used by Permission

THE IMPERIAL MARCH (DARTH VADER'S THEME)
© 1980 WARNER-TAMERLANE PUBLISHING CORP. and BANTHA MUSIC
All Rights Administered by WARNER-TAMERLANE PUBLISHING CORP.
All Rights Reserved   Used by Permission

DUEL OF THE FATES
from STAR WARS: EPISODE I - THE PHANTOM MENACE
Music by John Williams

Slowly

Double time

sostenuto

with gaining intensity

cresc. poco a poco

passionato

DUEL OF THE FATES
© 1999 BANTHA MUSIC
All Rights Administered by WARNER-TAMERLANE PUBLISHING CORP.
All Rights Reserved   Used by Permission